Using Kindle Fire HD

Kevin Wilson

Apress®

Using Kindle Fire HD

ISBN-13 (pbk): 978-1-4842-0581-5

ISBN-13 (electronic): 978-1-4842-0580-8

Publisher: Welmoed Spahr
Lead Editor: Steve Anglin
Development Editor: Jeff Pepper
Editorial Board: Steve Anglin, Ewan Buckingham, Gary Cornell, Louise Corrigan, James T. DeWolf, Jonathan Gennick, Robert Hutchinson, Michelle Lowman, James Markham, Matthew Moodie, Jeff Olson, Jeffrey Pepper, Douglas Pundick, Ben Renow-Clarke, Dominic Shakeshaft, Gwenan Spearing, Steve Weiss
Coordinating Editor: Melissa Maldonado
Copy Editor: Mary Behr
Compositor: SPi Global
Indexer: SPi Global
Artist: SPi Global
Cover Designer: Anna Ishchenko

Distributed to the book trade worldwide by Springer Science+Business Media New York, 233 Spring Street, 6th Floor, New York, NY 10013. Phone 1-800-SPRINGER, fax (201) 348-4505, e-mail orders-ny@springer-sbm.com, or visit www.springeronline.com. Apress Media, LLC is a California LLC and the sole member (owner) is Springer Science + Business Media Finance Inc (SSBM Finance Inc). SSBM Finance Inc is a Delaware corporation.

For information on translations, please e-mail rights@apress.com, or visit www.apress.com.

Apress and friends of ED books may be purchased in bulk for academic, corporate, or promotional use. eBook versions and licenses are also available for most titles. For more information, reference our Special Bulk Sales–eBook Licensing web page at www.apress.com/bulk-sales.

Any source code or other supplementary materials referenced by the author in this text is available to readers at www.apress.com. For detailed information about how to locate your book's source code, go to www.apress.com/source-code/.

Contents at a Glance

Contents

About the Author

Kevin Wilson, a practicing computer engineer and tutor, has had a passion for gadgets, cameras, computers and technology for many years.

After graduating with a masters in computer science, software engineering and multimedia systems, he has worked in the computer industry supporting and working with many different types of computer systems. He has also served as an IT Tutor in education running specialist lessons on film making, visual effects and computer literacy for young people. He has taught in colleges in South Africa and as a tutor for adult education in England.
He has produced a number of guides similar to this one designed to give people a quick basic knowledge of the book's topic.

Preface

The Kindle Fire is a mini tablet computer that offers a unique feature set for those interested in a tablet with excellent color, quite readable screens for books and other documents and an array of other features. This book is meant to be a fast introduction to the Fire for those who might want to purchase one or who want to know how to master its features. The book proceeds quickly with lots of visuals so that you can learn what you need to know with a minimal investment in time. An attempt has been made to answer the basic questions that users may experience while walking you through the generally used tasks.

The book starts by discussing the features of the Fire, the various formats, the main screen, and setting up the Fire. Thereafter, you will learn the basic gestures used to move on the screen to round out your basic knowledge of how to get around on the device.

You will learn how to work with the cloud to store your movies, books games, pictures and music. The book then gives walk throughs so that you know how to use each of these features. For those with children, you will learn how to protect your children from unwanted content.

Thereafter the book shows you how to access the Internet using the Silk browser and how to create "bookmarks" for your favorites. It then goes on to discuss loading your email system and using email on the Fire, using Calendar and using Skype for messaging. It continues with sections on watching videos and using YouTube on your Fire and concludes with tutorials on different ways of adding files to your device.

The book is meant to impart the most information in as few words as possible. It uses graphics so show every step along the way. This book will truly have you running effectively on your Fire in no time.

Chapter 1

Introduction

The Kindle Fire is a mini tablet computer from Amazon.com. It comes in various different versions and sizes (prices subject to change):

- Fire HD 6: 8GB @ $99 with a 6-inch display

- Fire HD 6: 16GB @ $199 with a 6-inch display

- Fire HD 7: 8GB @ $139 with a 7-inch display

- Fire HD 7: 16GB @ $159 with a 7-inch display

- Kindle Fire HDX: 16B @ $199; upgradable to FireOS 4

- Fire HDX 8.9: 16GB @ $379; 4G version is $479, with FireOS 4

- Fire HD Kids Edition, which has a quite liberal replacement policy and superior child controls

The Kindle Fire models are known for their excellent screen resolution, durability (with Gorilla Glass displays on the HD models), long-lasting batteries, and speedy Wi-Fi connections. Their size and weight are well engineered for your hand. The sound on the new HDX is significantly louder than on the iPad and is clear, even, and crisp even at max volume. Here are just some of the features available:

- You can access the Internet using the Silk web browser and check your e-mail using the e-mail app.

- You can download from a large library of books straight to your Kindle and read them everywhere you go. The screens have the clean appearance of the Amazon Kindle devices.

- You can connect with social media such as Facebook and Twitter to engage with your friends, and take photos with the built-in camera and post them directly to your Facebook or Twitter pages.

- You can download and watch movies and connect your Kindle to your TV and watch them on a big screen.

- You can choose from a variety of games available in the App Store.

- You can download your favorite music from the Music Store or off your computer straight to your Kindle.

- Amazon's new Family Library feature allows you to share your games, books, videos, and apps with others in your home even if they have different Amazon accounts.

- Using Amazon Workspaces on your HDX, you can even run Windows 8 from the cloud on your tablet, meaning for instance that you have access to your Windows-based business apps on your Fire HDX.

- You can even keep your kids safe with the built-in parental controls that allows you to monitor or block content.

In the rest of this book, you will explore how to use the Fire, its features, and how the significant software works so that you are well equipped to use your Fire successfully.

Chapter 2

Initial Setup

This chapter will cover the basics of the initial setup.

Powering On

Power on your device by pressing the small button on the bottom of your Kindle.

Once the device has started up, you will see the lock screen. Slide the lock with your finger to open your Kindle. The first time you start up your device you will need to register it with Amazon.

If you purchased your Kindle from Amazon, it will already be registered to you so you will not have to register it again.

Connecting to Wi-Fi

First, select your Wi-Fi from the list of wireless networks detected.
Your network name (SSID) and password (network key) is usually printed
on a sticker on the back of your router, DSL, or cable modem.

Enter the network key when prompted.

Registering Your Kindle

Set the time zones to the closest city in your time zone and then tap
continue.

Enter your Amazon account details. If you don't have an Amazon account, click the Create an account link and follow the instructions to sign up.

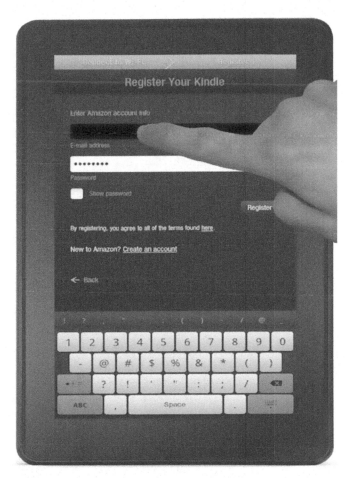

When you are done, tap the Register button. This links your Kindle to your Amazon account. All Kindle purchases will be paid for using your Amazon account payment details and delivered to your Kindle.

You can also add your Facebook or Twitter account. On the confirmation screen, click the Get started now link.

Go make yourself a cup of coffee and start using your Kindle.

Chapter **3**

The Kindle Fire

As discussed earlier, the Kindle Fire is an enhanced functionality mini tablet version of the Kindle e-book reader from Amazon and, as of this date, has a color, 6 to 8.9 inch, multi-touch screen and runs an Android operating system called Fire OS.

The device includes access to the Amazon App Store where you can purchase apps, games, books, magazines, and music as well as stream movies and TV shows straight to your Kindle.

Understanding the Home Screen

The main start screen on the Kindle Fire is shown below. It has a status bar at the top and a search field below that (enabling you to search your Kindle or the Web). The content stored on your Kindle is broken down into categories on the navigation bar. A carousel keeps a history list of all the content you have accessed on your Kindle.

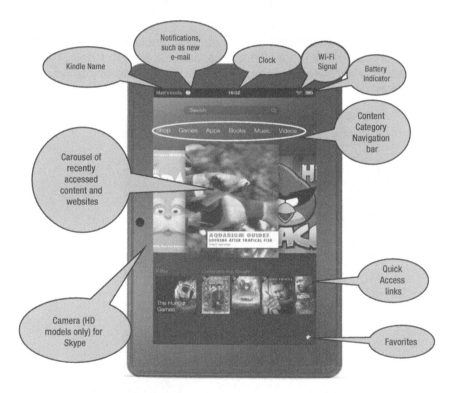

Search: Tapping on the Search field allows you to enter you search term(s) so that you can search your content libraries or the Web.

Content Navigation Bar: You can access the Web or your content libraries at the top of the home screen by tapping on the names in your Content Navigation Bar and swiping your finger to go through them: Shop, Games, Apps, Books, Music, Videos, Newsstand, Audiobooks, the Web, Photos, Docs, and Offers.

Carousel: The Carousel contains recently used apps, web pages, videos, music, books, music, newspapers, and magazines as they are automatically added to the carousel. You can swipe your finger to scroll through the Carousel where the most recent items appear first for convenience.

Favorites: For the selected content type, you are able to view your favorites will appear in your library.

Ports and Buttons

On the side of the HD version of the Kindle you will see two ports. One is a Micro USB port for charging and connecting to a computer. The other is a Micro HDMI port to connect to an HDMI-capable TV or projector, which allows you to watch movies and videos.

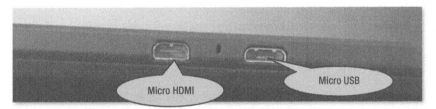

On the other edge of the tablet are the power button, volume control buttons, and a 1/8-inch headphone jack.

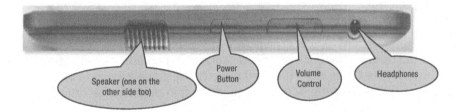

To turn your Kindle on: Press the power button once.

To send your Kindle to sleep mode: Press the power button once.

To completely shut down your Kindle: Press and hold the power button for 3 seconds and then tap Shut down.

The Options Bar

The options bar can be found at the bottom of most screens.

Here is a brief explanation of each icon:

⌂	**Home**	Tap this button to go back to the home screen.
←	**Back**	Tap this to go to the previous screen.
☰	**Menu**	Tap this to view the menu options for the current screen.
◯	**Search**	Tap this to search your libraries (music, books, photos, etc.) as well as the Internet.
★	**Favorites**	Tap this to view apps, books, games, etc. marked as favorites.

To access the options bar if it disappears while using an app or watching a video, swipe your finger from the right edge or the screen (if using in landscape orientation) or the bottom edge (if using in portrait orientation). The menu will appear.

If you are reading a book in full screen, tap on the page to reveal the menu.

The Navigation Bar (Libraries)

Your libraries are displayed at the top of your Home screen in the navigation bar.

Tap the library name to see all the available content within that library.

hop   Games   Apps   Books   Music   Videos   Newsstand   Audiobooks   Web

Chapter 4

The Settings Menu

The Settings menu is hidden but can be activated by swiping your finger down from the top edge of the screen.

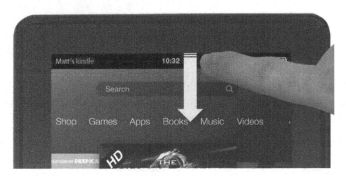

This will reveal the Settings menu.

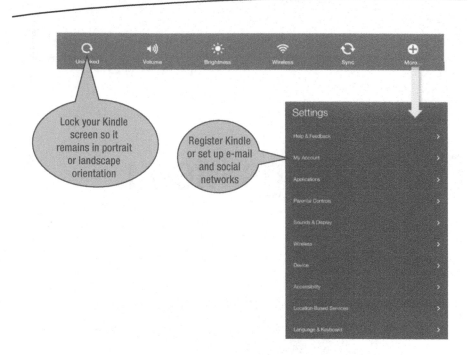

Here you can lock the screen orientation, change the volume or brightness, set up your Wi-Fi, and sync your content with Amazon's cloud. The following are the most common options and settings:

- Tapping More will give you more options.

- Help & Feedback: Gives you access to Amazon customer service, Getting Started Guides, etc.

- My Account: Allows you to register your Kindle to your Amazon account, and add Facebook, Twitter, and e-mail accounts.

- Applications: Shows you what is installed on your Kindle.

- Parental Controls: Allows you to set up your Kindle if you have children who use it. You can block websites, restrict time, restrict applications they can use, block inappropriate videos, disable Wi-Fi, etc.

- Sounds & Display: Allows you to set volume levels, screen brightness levels, and assign sound effects to notifications such as incoming e-mail, etc.

- Wireless: Allows you to connect to a wireless network, and enable Bluetooth connections.

■ Device: Gives you information about what is stored on your Kindle, plus the amount of storage available and storage used. It shows the battery life remaining and allows you to set the date and time.

■ Accessibility: Allows you to enable the voice guide that speaks the names of headings and reads aloud what is displayed on your Kindle. It also allows you to lock the orientation to portrait or landscape mode so it doesn't change automatically.

■ Location-Based Services: Allows you to enable GPS location to determine your physical location. This is useful when using maps, and to help your Kindle find local points of interest.

■ Language & Keyboard: Allows you to change the onscreen keyboard depending on your locality. For example, you can set it to UK or US or your native language. Note that you can purchase a keyboard from Amazon for your Kindle Fire that works with devices other than the Fire.

■ Security: Allows you to set lock screen passwords to secure your Kindle. I will cover this in detail later in the book.

Chapter 5

Using Your Kindle

By now, you're familiar with tapping to select buttons and other items on your Kindle Fire, as shown in the previous chapters.

You can also use several other gestures to interact with your Kindle Fire. This chapter will show the basic gestures that you are likely to use daily.

In addition to tapping to select items, you can zoom in on a figure in a book or a web site, as shown on the following page. There you can see that by pinching the screen you can zoom in or out.

Zoom into web page by pinching the screen.

Tip Cancelling a Tap

Taps are registered when you lift your finger from the screen. If you tap something by mistake and you want to cancel the tap, slide your finger onto another part of the screen before lifting it.

Slide your finger across the screen to scroll up and down a web site or document.

Swipe the carousel left and right to navigate. Tap to select.

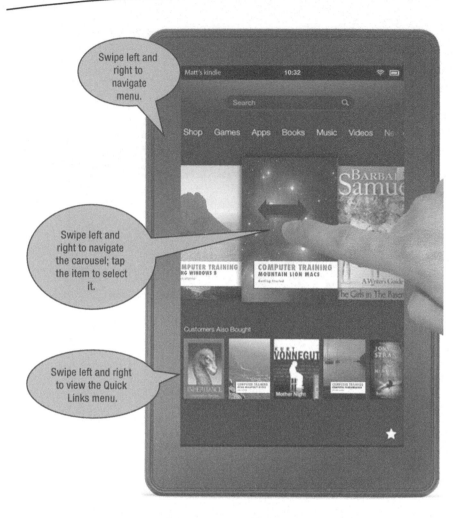

You can also tap and hold your finger on an item and a context menu will appear.

The Add to Playlist option adds the selected track to a new playlist. In this way you can queue up a list of tracks to play one after the other. The Shop this Artist option allows you to search Amazon's music store for more tracks and albums by the same artist. The Remove from Device option deletes the track off your Kindle, but it will still be available on your Amazon account (in the cloud).

Organizing the Home Screen

You can utilize the Favorites shelves below the carousel to add some of your most accessed content. You can edit the shelves in three ways: add, remove or rearrange.

To add an icon to the shelf, tap and hold your finger on an item you want in the Carousel, and in the menu that appears, select Add to Favorites.

To remove an icon from the shelf, tap and hold your finger on the icon and select Remove from Favorites from the menu that appears.

If you want to rearrange the icons in your Favorites shelves, tap and hold your finger on the icon and drag it to the desired spot.

Chapter **6**

Device and Cloud Storage

Any content you purchase from Amazon for you Kindle is securely stored remotely on Amazon's servers; the content is said to be stored in the cloud and so it is known as cloud storage. The idea is to allow you to access your content from anywhere, not just on your home computer or Kindle. So if for instance you happened to have a problem with your device you could still retain your data.

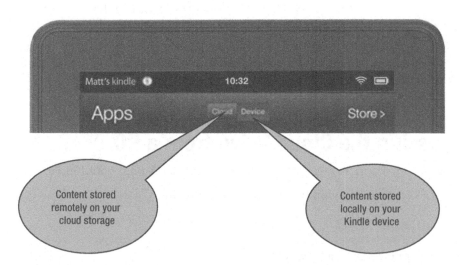

All your music, books, newspapers, and apps are stored on the cloud storage and are synched or copied to your device. Depending on your Kindle, you get anywhere between 4GB and 16GB of storage on your Kindle.

*Music, photos, documents, and books are all
stored remotely on Amazon's Cloud Drive.*

Cloud Drive

Cloud Drive is an online storage service that allows you to store files such as music, photos, and documents. At the time of writing, you get 5GB free on the Cloud Drive. Then you can get 20GB for $10 a year and 50GB for $25 a year.

Files can be stored on your Kindle and on the Cloud Drive. Using the Cloud Drive app, you can easily transfer files from your PC to your Kindle and vice versa.

Accessing the Cloud Drive from a PC

The Cloud Drive app allows you to copy files from a PC onto your Kindle.

On your PC, open your web browser and navigate to

http://www.amazon.com/gp/drive/app-download

In the prompt that appears, click Run.

This will guide you through the installation process. Once installed, you can find your Cloud Drive in Favorites in Windows Explorer.

Click the Cloud Drive icon to show your files on your Cloud Drive, as shown below.

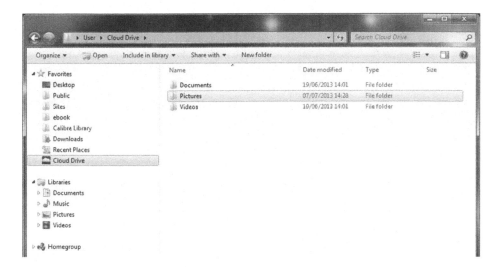

You can drag and drop files in to the folders or delete them, as shown in the right-hand pane. Just copy them from your libraries.

Securing Your Fire

If you are like most people, you will have data on your device that you would not like to lose or be stolen. If this is the case, it is a good idea to secure your device with a password.   Otherwise, your Fire could end up in the wrong hands and all of your content would be available to whomever found it.

To set a password, swipe your finger down from the top of the screen to reveal the Settings menu, tap More, then tap Security, and turn the Lock screen password on.

Chapter 7

Games and Apps

You can view your "apps", that is, your Fire software applications, including games, by tapping Apps on the home screen.

This will display all the apps currently installed. To open an app, tap its icon.

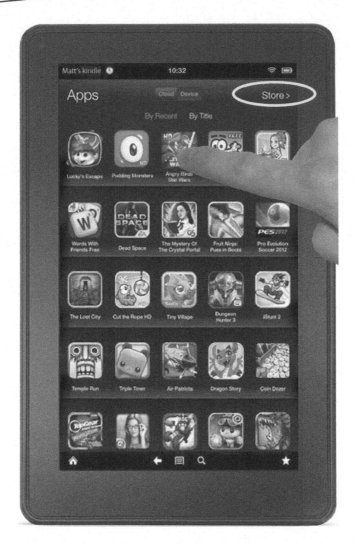

You can purchase apps on your Kindle Fire by tapping Store in the top right corner of the Apps library screen as circled on the screen shown here.

Here, you can get both paid apps and free apps. You can browse the top paid and free apps, and search the App Store by tapping in the Search in App Store field and using the keyboard to enter the app name you are looking for.

You can explore content categories such as New, Games, Entertainment, and Lifestyle.

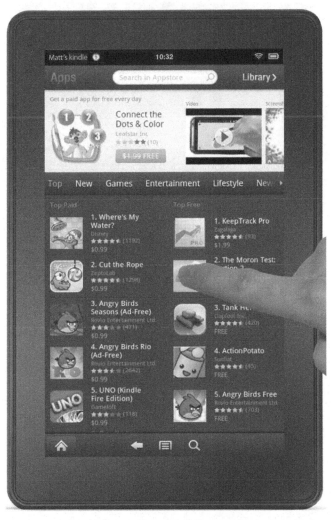

To buy an app, select the app, tap the orange price button and confirm your purchase by pressing the green Buy App button. The app will be downloaded, installed, and placed in your Apps library.

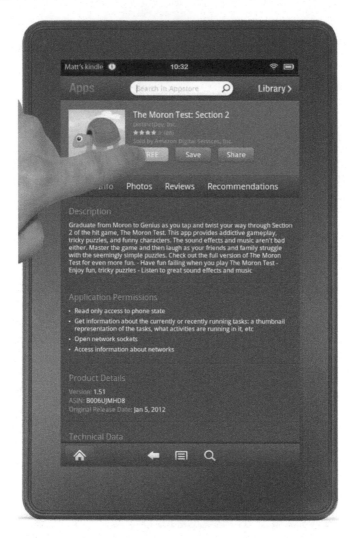

Tap the app icon in your Apps library to open it up.

From time to time you will probably decide that you no longer wish to keep an app on your Kindle Fire.

If this is the case, you can uninstall it. Select Apps from the navigation bar on your home screen, tap and hold your finger on the app icon, and select Remove from Device from the menu that appears.

Apps can be paid for using the payment details you entered on your Amazon account.

Chapter 8

Books

You can view your books by tapping Books on the navigation menu on the home screen; this will display all the books purchased.

Tap a book cover to begin reading.

Sit back and enjoy reading your book!

If you want to browse the book store, tap Store on the top right of the book library screen.

Tap Search book store and, using the keyboard that appears, type in the author or book title you are looking for.

To view the book details, tap the book's front cover.

You can view a sample of the book by tapping Try a Sample. If you like the book, tap Buy to buy the book.

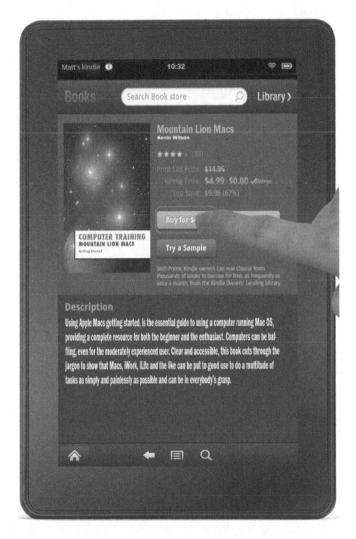

The book will be downloaded and added to your book library.

Chapter 9

Music

You can view your music collection by tapping Music on the navigation menu on the home screen. This will display all the albums imported or purchased.

From the Music library, you can browse your music by playlist, artist, album, individual song, or particular genre. In this example, I am playing a classical album.

To open an album, tap the album cover.

This takes you to the play screen where you can skip tracks, pause, and change the volume.

You can search for music at the Amazon MP3 store; to do so, simply tap Music from the home screen and then tap Store.

At the top, you will see the Amazon's featured MP3 deals and promotions. In addition, you can browse for music using the New Releases and Genres categories. Later in the book, I will discuss downloading music from your PC.

To search by artist, album, or track, type the name in the Search field (circled above). To purchase, tap the price button, and then tap Buy to confirm. That's it. Your 1-Click payment method will be charged automatically.

Chapter **10**

Photographs and the Camera

To access photos, tap Photos from the menu on the home screen. With Device selected, this will show all the photos you have on your Kindle, either ones you have uploaded from your Cloud Drive or Facebook, or ones you have taken with the on-board camera.

Tap your photograph to enlarge it.

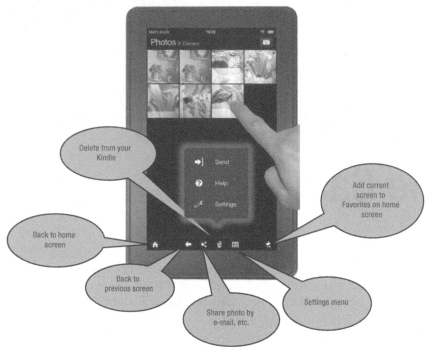

To connect to Facebook, tap Settings as shown above, then tap Add Photos, tap Facebook, then add Facebook photos. Enter your Facebook username and password and Kindle will sync your photos from Facebook albums.

To add photos to Facebook from the Kindle, tap on the photo you want to share, then tap the Settings menu as labelled above. Then on the Send dialog that appears, scroll down, dragging your finger over until you see Facebook. You can also save them to your Cloud Drive or e-mail them the same way, instead of or in addition to sending them to Facebook.

Built-in Camera

To access the built-in camera, tap Photos from your home screen, then tap the camera icon, as shown below.

To take a photo, tap the shutter icon, as highlighted below.

The camera is designed for video chat such as Skype, so taking a photograph can be quite tricky since it is a front-facing camera.

To share the photograph, tap the Settings menu and tap Send. Scroll down to Facebook if you want to share it on Facebook, or use e-mail, etc.

Chapter **11**

Browsing the Web

Amazon Silk is the name of the new web browser, run on Amazon Web Services (AWS), for the Kindle Fire. The Internet is accessed using the Wi-Fi connection you set up earlier in this book. You can connect to any Wi-Fi hotspot in the same way.

Simply tap Web on the navigation bar on the home screen to access Amazon Silk.

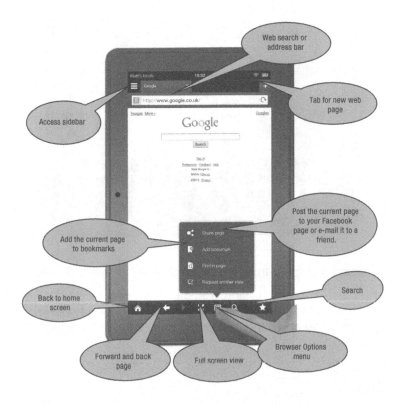

Web search or address bar

Tab for new web page

Access sidebar

Post the current page to your Facebook page or e-mail it to a friend.

Add the current page to bookmarks

Back to home screen

Search

Forward and back page

Full screen view

Browser Options menu

The sidebar is a new feature that allows you to quickly access bookmarks, browsing history, and your most visited web sites.

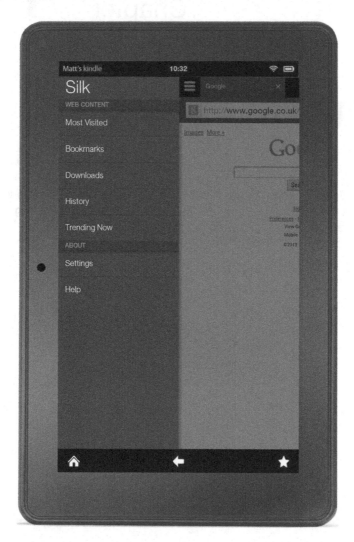

Quickly access the sidebar from the navigation bar on the Silk web browser.

Silk makes use of tabbed browsing. You can open new tabs for a web page by tapping the + on the top right; Silk will show you a list of your most visited web sites. You can either tap on the site or type in a search term in the Search box.

One feature I find really useful when browsing the Web on a Kindle is to use Silk's reader function.

You will find that this option appears in the address bar on most web sites. This feature displays a web page as if it were an e-book and makes reading much easier.

Bookmarks

You will probably want to bookmark your most visited web sites and files you have downloaded. They can all be accessed from the sidebar.

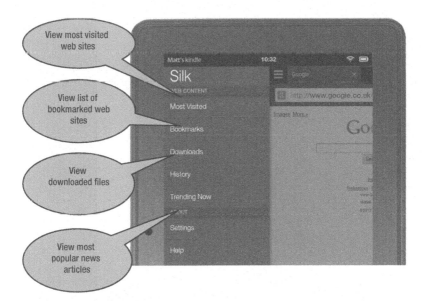

Bookmarking a site can be done using Silk's Options menu.

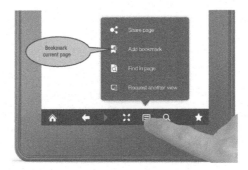

Chapter **12**

Setting up E-mail

The Kindle Fire contains an e-mail app allowing you to get your e-mail. You can launch the app by tapping the E-mail icon in the Apps library.

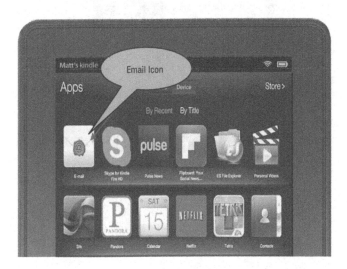

Kindle Fire e-mail supports Gmail, Yahoo Mail, Hotmail, and AOL. It also supports many other industry-standard IMAP and POP e-mail systems. So to use your existing account, you will want to set up your email account on the Fire.

To get started, tap the icon for the type of e-mail account you have. In this case, I am adding a Hotmail account, but the principle applies to the others as well.

53

Then type in your e-mail address, password, and a description (e.g., Hotmail account). You can also choose to make that address your default account so that any messages you send from your Fire will be from that address.

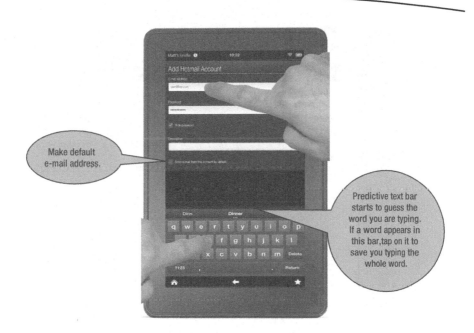

Make default e-mail address.

Predictive text bar starts to guess the word you are typing. If a word appears in this bar,tap on it to save you typing the whole word.

Not all of your email accounts may be free. You may receive a message telling you that you might have to pay for a premium or Plus subscription to get POP access to your e-mail. Most are still provided free (Gmail and Hotmail).

You can open an e-mail by tapping on it in your inbox, as shown below.

You can now access your e-mail at any time by tapping the e-mail icon in the Apps library.

Chapter 13

Calendar and Skype

You can access all your apps from the Apps menu on your main screen.

Keeping Appointments with Calendar

With the Calendar app, you can add new events or edit existing events.

To add a new event, double-tap an empty section at the time and date the appointment will take place, such as Thursday, September 6 at 12pm.

To edit an event, tap the event, and then tap Edit. To delete an event, tap the event, and then tap Delete.

You can choose to sort or display calendar events by list, day, week, or month.

Skype Your Friends

Skype allows you to instant message (chat) between users on Skype around the world. Tap Apps from the menu on the home screen and tap Skype.

You will need to sign in with either a Microsoft account or a Skype account. If you don't have one, tap Create a Skype Account and follow the directions.

Once you are in, give your friends your Skype account id or address and they can call you and have a video chat.

Skype is great way to keep in touch with family living in other countries or friends that live a long way from you. Plus, Skype is free and more personal than a phone call or e-mail.

To add a contact, tap the little contact icon shown below and enter their Skype id. This will add their name to your contact list. To call them, just tap on their name.

Chapter **14**

Watching Videos

You can watch videos and films you get from Amazon using a LoveFilm subscription. You can watch them on your Kindle screen or, if you prefer a more cinematic experience, you can hook up your Kindle Fire HD to your TV using a Micro HDMI cable. To do so, plug the large end into the back of your TV and the mini end into the side of your Kindle. Newer TVs will support HDMI.

Watch your film in glorious high definition.

The process for accessing videos is similar to the other applications we have discussed and we will use YouTube as an example in the following section. One area that may trip you up though is Flash. While Flash is supported by Silk, it is disabled by default despite being widely used still on the net. To enable Flash you need to use the Silk Settings menu. Then follow the directions to enable Flash.

If you haven't updated your Kindle Fire to the latest software version available, this setting can be accessed by tapping the Enable plug-ins option.

To update your Kindle Fire to the latest software version, visit

`http://www.amazon.com/Kindlesoftwareupdates`

YouTube

You can view YouTube videos on your Kindle Fire by opening up your web browser and browse to

`http://m.youtube.com`

Then you can tap the magnifying glass icon to search for a video.

When watching videos, they look better if you have your Kindle in landscape orientation.

If you have connected your Kindle to your HD-ready TV, you can watch these videos on a big screen.

To close your video, swipe your finger across the screen from the right edge and tap the back icon.

YouTube App

You can also download a YouTube app free from the App Store. Just search for "YouTube" in the App Store.

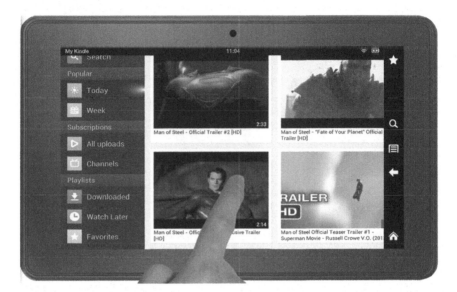

Chapter 15

Adding Your Music

One of Kindle's many functions is the capability to stream or download music from your Amazon Cloud Drive. Go to the following web site on your computer and sign in:

`http://www.amazon.com/cloudplayer`

Uploading From Your PC

Go to the Amazon MP3 page and click the Cloud Player banner in the upper-right corner.

Sign in with your Amazon account and click the Import your music option from the upper-left corner and then click the Download Now button to download the MP3 Uploader.

Once downloaded, open the Uploader and follow the instructions to install it.

Once installed, the Uploader will scan your computer's hard drive for MP3s to upload. After scanning finishes, select the MP3s you want uploaded and click the Start upload button.

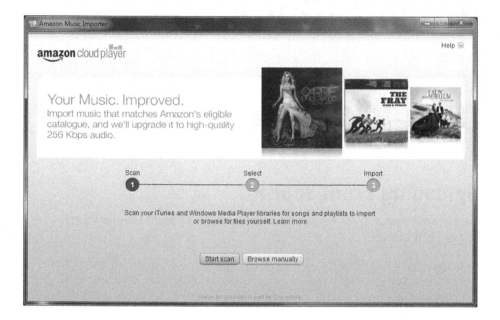

Depending on how much music you have to upload, this may take a while, so go make a cup of coffee (or tea if you prefer).

If you have a large amount of music on your machine, it is best to select Edit Selections.

This gives you the option of manually selecting the music you want on your Kindle. Choose wisely; you only have 250-song capacity on the free cloud.

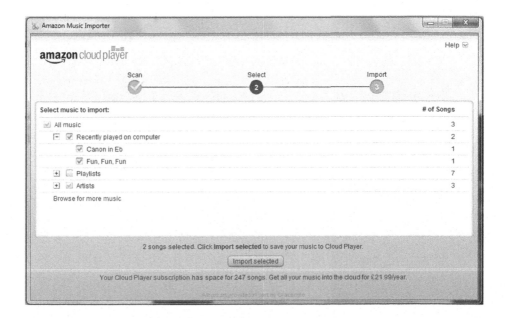

You will get a warning when you are near your limit.

Finding Music on Your Kindle Fire

Make sure you've signed in with the Amazon account for the music you just uploaded and tap the Music tab. Then tap the Cloud tab.

There you'll see your uploaded music. If you're on a Wi-Fi connection, you can either tap a song to stream it or tap and hold your finger on the screen for a few seconds to download it to your Kindle.

If you uploaded quite a few songs, reveal the Settings menu by swiping your finger down from the top of the screen and tap Sync.

Once downloaded, you can access your songs in your Music library by tapping Device and finding them there.

Chapter 16

Parental Controls

The parental controls allow you to seal off access (through password protection) to areas on your Fire that you may not want people to access at a somewhat granular level. Obviously, children are a significant target of this protection, but this area allows you to prevent access to specific areas such as email or your contacts to other people who you might allow on your device. To access this area, on your home screen, swipe down from the top edge to reveal the settings bar.

Tap More.

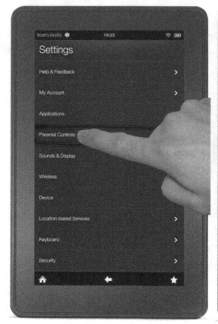 

Then select the Parental Controls option. Enter a password and then you can modify the Parental Control settings on your Fire.

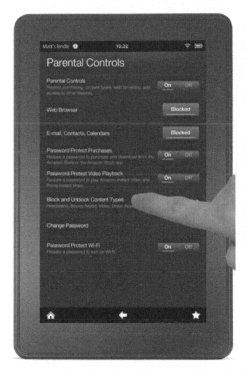 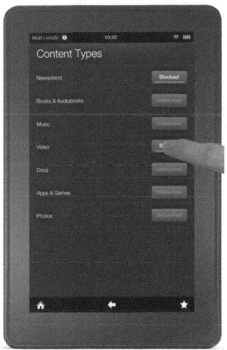

From this menu, you can password protect features such as your web browser, email, videos, music, your photos, your documents, access to Wi-Fi or purchasing content on Amazon.com. So these features are not just for kids.

Blocking certain types of content from the Parental Controls screen will remove that item from the Kindle navigation bar at the top of the home screen.

After you have made your selections, tap the back arrow in the lower part of the Parental Controls menu.

Kindle FreeTime

The Kindle Store offers a wide array of content that may or may not be suitable or of any interest for your children. Kindle FreeTime is designed to enable access to age-appropriate content for your children. The best part is you can set up six users on your Fire. So you can have different settings for each of your children if you wish.

Amazon's Kindle FreeTime app makes this possible by allowing you to set up a library of content that's educational and appropriate for different age ranges.

The content in the FreeTime library is free to FreeTime subscribers.

Each child sees only the books, videos, and apps in the FreeTime library and any additional content you added.

You can't exit the Kindle FreeTime app without the Parental Controls password. This prevents them from accessing other content on the Kindle Fire without your permission.

Daily Time Limits

Another nice feature of FreeTime is it gives parents the ability to set daily time limits for reading books, watching TV shows and movies, and using apps. As you can imagine, this is a huge plus for parents who want to limit game time to an hour or two a day without affecting their child's desire to read for hours on end.

Setting Up FreeTime and Adding Content

To set up FreeTime, download the app from the Amazon Store and tap on it to launch.

Enter your Parental Controls password. Then create a user account, input all the necessary information, and tap Next. You can add up to six profiles.

Tap the photo box to add a photo or picture to the profile.

Enter your child's name in the text box, select their gender and birthday, and tap Next at the bottom of the screen. Your child's profile is complete.

Once the profile is created, you can open FreeTime and tap your child's profile image to put the Kindle Fire HD in FreeTime mode.

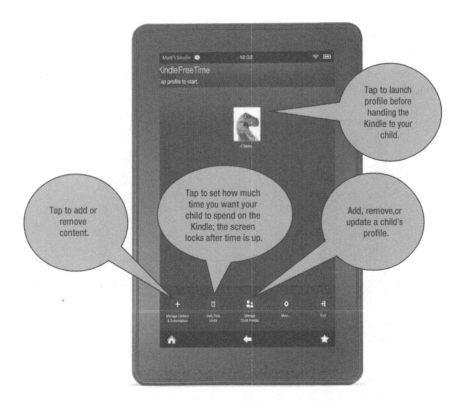

To manually add content to your child's profile, launch the FreeTime app and tap Manage Content & Subscription at the bottom of the page.

Enter your password and tap Manage Your Content. You can then view and manage a list of the books, videos, and apps that you own on your account. From this screen, you can tap the item you want to make available on their FreeTime account.

Once FreeTime is running in the background, your children can't leave the application without entering the Parental Controls password, so you should keep this password a secret.

Setting the Daily Time Limits

As mentioned before, FreeTime also allows you to limit the amount of time your child can use the Kindle.

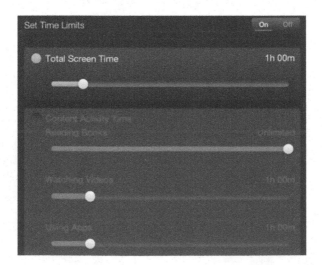

To choose daily time limits, tap Total Screen Time and move the slider to the appropriate amount of time you want your child to use the Kindle.

You can also put a limit on different content types. To restrict each specific content type, select Content Activity Time and then set the amount of time you want your child to be able to read books, watch videos, or use apps.

Tap the back arrow to save your settings.

Chapter **17**

Sending Documents to the Kindle

Documents can be sent to your Kindle by e-mailing them to your Kindle email address. The email address is on your Amazon account page. Alternatively, you can add files directly by connecting the Kindle to your computer.

Now, Amazon offers a Windows/ Mac application, Send to Kindle, which provides a simple solution for you to send documents from your PC to your Kindle Fire. On Windows, you simply right click from Windows Explorer. You can also send a document from any Windows program by choosing print, then selecting Send to Kindle as a printer option. This chapter will discuss how to set up Send to Kindle and discuss all of the file sending options in more detail.

Installation

Go to the following website, download and install the Send to Kindle program on your PC with Windows 7 and 8 or Mac OS.

http://www.amazon.com/sendtokindle/pc

You will be asked to register Send to Kindle, and you will enter your Amazon account e-mail address, the password, and click the Register button.

Sending from Windows Explorer

In Windows Explorer on your PC, right-click on a document you want to send to your Kindle, and select Send to Kindle.

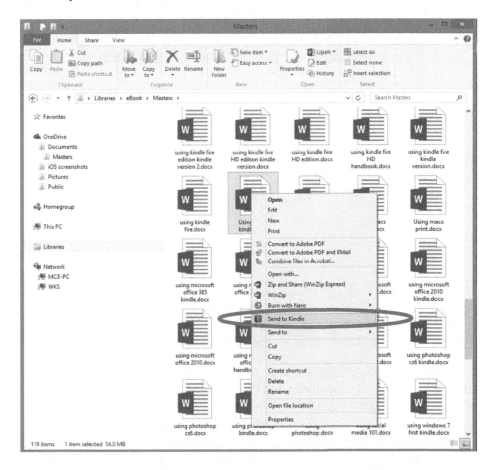

If you want to send more than one document, you can select files while holding down the **Ctrl** key. Then when you have them selected, click Send to Kindle.

This may take a few minutes; check your Kindle to see if your documents have been delivered. Document and graphic file types such as .doc, .jpeg, and so on (other than PDF) will be converted automatically to Kindle format.

You may need to sync your Kindle if your documents do not go through. You can do this by going to the Settings menu and tapping on Sync. The maximum file size is 50 MB and if you are storing your documents on the Amazon Cloud, you have 5GBs of storage space.

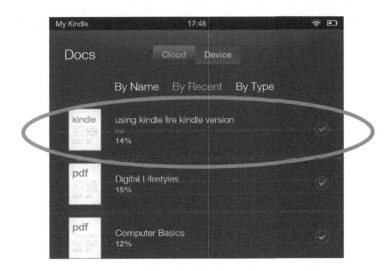

Sending from a Print Dialog

To send a document from a Windows program, select Print, and then choose Send to Kindle as your printer from the drop down menu.

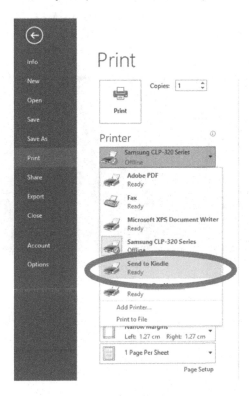

When the Send to Kindle window pops up, you will need to select from the options on the screen shown below and then click the Send button.

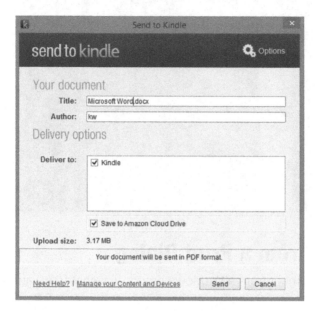

Once you click send, your file will be uploaded to Amazon cloud and you will be able to download it to your Kindle. You can find your document in the docs section on the menu.

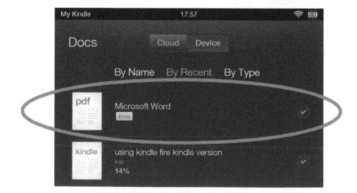

Adding Files Using Explorer

If you plug your Kindle into your computer, you can access it using Windows Explorer as shown below (Mac users can find it in the Finder window).

Caution   Do not mess with any of the directories here as you can seriously mess up your Kindle. I would suggest you keep to the following directories:

Documents

Music

Pictures

Videos

Leave the rest alone!

To get started, Open Windows Explorer by clicking your Explorer icon in the task bar. Scroll down to the Computer section in the Windows Explorer window.

In the left-hand pane you should see Libraries. This is where Windows stores all your personal files.

Note that in the Libraries section you see the four directories in the Caution at the start of this section.

Further down the left-hand pane, under Computer, you should see Kindle. If you open this up, you will see all the directories common to your computer and your Kindle device.

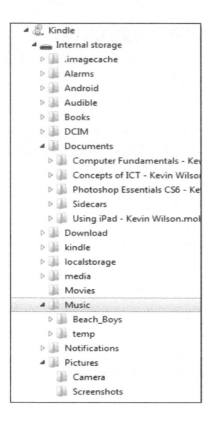

Adding a File

You can find files in your Libraries section in Windows Explorer. For example, click your Music library, and then from the right-hand pane, drag the file you want from your computer's Music section into the Music folder representing your Kindle. It helps to arrange your windows as shown below so that you can see the Kindle directories.

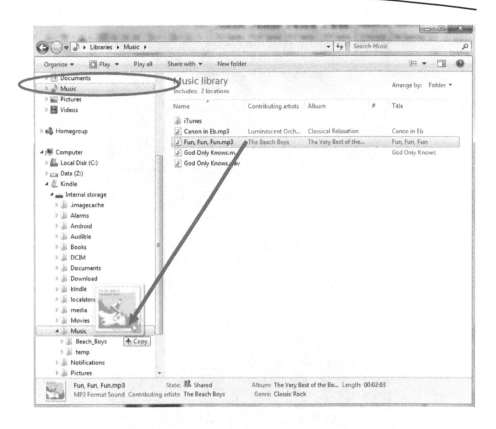

Once you are done, you can find the newly added track in the Music library on your device, as shown below.

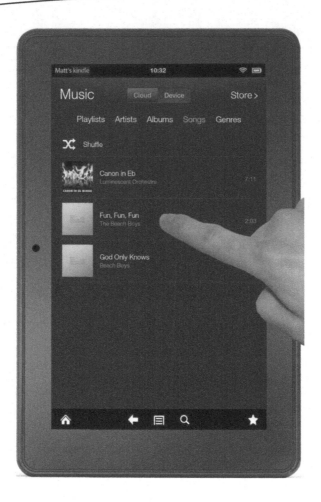

You can do the same for pictures and documents.

Index

Get the eBook for only $10!

Now you can take the weightless companion with you anywhere, anytime. Your purchase of this book entitles you to 3 electronic versions for only $10.

This Apress title will prove so indispensible that you'll want to carry it with you everywhere, which is why we are offering the eBook in 3 formats for only $10 if you have already purchased the print book.

Convenient and fully searchable, the PDF version enables you to easily find and copy code—or perform examples by quickly toggling between instructions and applications. The MOBI format is ideal for your Kindle, while the ePUB can be utilized on a variety of mobile devices.

Go to www.apress.com/promo/tendollars to purchase your companion eBook.